Also by Douglas Worth

Of Earth (1974)
Invisibilities (1977)

TRIPTYCH

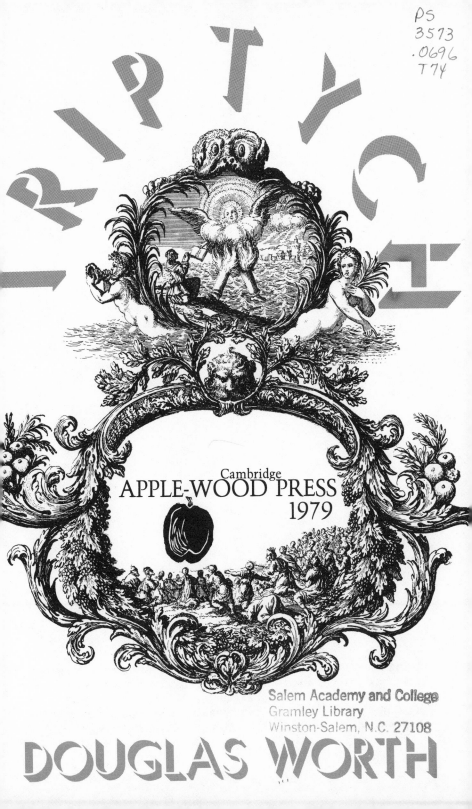

Cambridge
APPLE-WOOD PRESS
1979

DOUGLAS WORTH

TRIPTYCH

DOUGLAS WORTH

Acknowledgments

The author would like to thank the editors of the following publications in which some of these poems previously appeared: Aspect, Boston Herald American, Invisibilities (Apple-wood Press), New American Poetry (McGraw-Hill), Of Earth (William L. Bauhan, Publisher), Poem, Sparrow, The Newton Times, and Meadowbrook Newsletter.

For their scientific guidance and philosophical inspiration, the author wishes to acknowledge the indebtedness of *Song of One World* to Victor Weisskopf's *Knowledge and Wonder* and Richard Leakey's *Origins*.

CONTENTS

65   III   SONG OF ONE WORLD

I

GUESTS IN EDEN
A One-Act Chamber Opera
(for Peter Schickele)

I: DAWN

(The curtain rises on Eden. It is dawn, the first light just
filtering through the darkness. Adam can be seen, dimly,
lying asleep. God enters and regards him for a time. He is
just about to begin His day of rest, having completed the
Creation, and, most recently, Adam, who has not yet
awakened to the world.)

God   (approaches Adam, stands over him, then kneels, as the
song progresses.)

He is still sleeping
peacefully, his face
turned toward the brightening, gleams
as if with its own dim light
as I approach.

So like a god
immaculate, he seems
almost too perfect
for mortality,
his rose mouth fit for hymns
of near-angelic
harmony and grace,
yet sensual, keen
with its lush slidings, chiseled teeth
for the more savage work
of animals.

Curled on themselves, his hands
like petals, acorns
gathering force—
what acts
of infinite precision, reach
ordering chaos
holocaust, may spring
out of their delicate
awakening?

I smooth a curl back
brush the silky bloom
of his warm, sleep-flushed cheek—
his eyes flicker open
blindly, close, absorbed
in dreamwork, bloodwork
flowing beyond my grasp
around the bones
that will support the flowering
of his life
a little while, then fold
and crumble back
to the unconscious
dust from which they rose.

Drawn down by love and fear
for what I have created
in my own image, grown
mysterious and distant
on his own,
ignorant, helpless, and responsible
I bend and gently plant
upon his brow a trembling
kiss of choice.

(God withdraws. As the light gradually increases, Adam
wakes and sits up, observing everything around him
with wonder, then rises and walks slowly about, groping
for names, for speech...)

Adam   stillness

the grass

heavy

the tree

waiting

to sing

the bud

folded

aware

the air

too rich

for touch

II: MORNING

Adam (walks in the garden by a stream, taking in everything with his senses, savoring and praising. Everything is bathed in a fresh, golden morning light, except the tree of knowledge, which is shadowy, darkly shining.)

Apricot, plum, orange, peach
exploding nectars, while from each
drunk branch an iridescent throat
brimmed with sweet fire, pours its note,
and roses, lilies, spreading their
ambrosias through the morning air
lift moist silk and velvet lips
to kiss my cheeks and fingertips—
every taste, touch, smell, sound, sight
feasts my senses with delight,
and, to sauce this luscious scene
of rich perfections, a soft sheen
of gold light, like pure happiness,
shines from each wonder—all, that is
except the apple! that one fruit God
forbade! its darkly lucent globe
is poisonous, He said; if I
should pluck and eat it, I would die
and Eden's beauty shrivel, spoiled...
I will not think such things!...yet, coiled
in shadow, something undefined,
some stirring, without tongue yet, blind,
hidden, here, within my breast
and here, still sleeping, in this nest
of warmth and peace, some seedlike urge
lies waiting, darkly, to emerge.
But what? Well, it's beyond me. Here
I'll rest and listen to the clear
untroubled music of this stream
that asks no further than the gleam
of sunlight, singing through its days:
it is enough to be, and praise.

(He lies down by the stream and falls asleep.)

III: NOON

(God enters and creates Eve from the sleeping Adam's rib,
then retires. Adam wakes to find her sleeping beside him.
He begins to sing, sitting beside her, and then, after
"What then when she awakes?" stands up.)

Adam   Is this some creature, or a fallen star
shimmering here beside me? flesh and hair,
limbs, features, very close to mine, yet far
more softly lustrous, rounded, rosed, and fair
beyond all telling—even as she lies
asleep, her tender beauty might command
the moon, to be her mirror, from the skies,
drunk with her image, hovering at her hand.
What then when she awakes? I feel a strange
presentiment of changes no defense
of mine could stand against or rearrange,
a radiant bliss, mixed with a darker sense
of loss and ending—what shall I conceive
to name this light in growing darkness? "Eve!"

Eve   (waking, looks around, sits up, and sees Adam.)

My Lord, for lord you seem
of this still-waking dream,
please tell me, if you can,
who, where, and what I am—
I have a memory
of some dark, endless sea
of silence, then a dim
seed of light, at the brim
of the horizon, grew
and slowly flowering, drew
me closer, till I heard
light singing, then a word
that called me, rose and broke
over me, and I woke—
but to what, or why, I came
my nature, or my name
I can't say...

Adam   You are Eve,
sent to me, I believe,

to share and make complete
this Eden, that was sweet
before you, but not filled
with such grace, brimmed and spilled
by your least movement. Lord,
and servant to your word,
I, Adam, welcome you
who have made myself two,
so close we seem—but what
we're here for, I cannot
say either, except to praise
the great Creator's ways.
I had a shadowy fear
of some change, drawing near...
but that's drowned in your eyes—
queen of the garden, rise!

(Taking Adam's hand, Eve rises. They stand and look at each other.)

Adam   you stand, wearing sunlight
around you
the world dissolving...

Eve   you stand, like the sun
around you
the world revolving...

(They sing this, again, together, their words intertwined, and then exchange a first, light kiss and innocent embrace.)

IV: AFTERNOON

Eve   (walks in the garden, holding an orange and a rose, near
the tree of knowledge, where the serpent waits.)

Queen of the garden. Queen! Can it be so?
Queen of this orange? Yes! My feelings flow
more richly than its juice, when I'm with him.
Queen of this rose? The texture of my skin
is softer, and more silky, to his touch.
Queen of the lark? My throat is filled with such
sweet music, when we talk. Queen of the deer?
My senses are more quick, when he comes near.
I am indeed queen here! Then why not queen
of more? Queen of the moon! Its lustrous sheen
is less, in Adam's eyes. Queen of the sun!
I'm Adam's queen, and Adam is my sun.
Queen of the sky, of the most distant star,
of the whole universe, queen!

Serpent   Lady, you are!
the moment you choose to pluck and eat this fruit
of darkly glimmering knowledge. Hear my suit!
One taste, and all this garden would appear
a passing dream, a shadow, in the clear
light of awareness: all that is, has been,
and might be, would be yours, and you its queen!

Eve   No! Adam forbade it! I must not
violate his command. But, tell me, what
are you?

Serpent   the flowering seed of your desire
to change and grow, reaching up, ever higher,
through knowledge and wonder, into the unknown...
I do not tempt you for yourself alone—
Adam himself is subject to some fear
of his true nature, that would keep him here
cloaked in its power. But you can free him, give
him the gift of knowledge, and both live
as gods, rising above your present curse
of ignorance, to embrace the universe!

If you refuse this chance, others, less sweet
May come, instead, to pluck...

Eve No! I will eat!

(She plucks an apple, and eats.)

that shiver
and flood of wreckage
light, the blind
beak piercing the shell

V: EVENING

(Adam sits by a tree, weaving a crown of roses, finishes it, and places it gently on his head. The late afternoon light gradually diminishes to darkness as the scene progresses.)

Adam How long I have been waiting for her now
to meet me, by this tree, feeling the slow
afternoon shadows stretch, imagining each
faint sound was her, approaching, with a peach
or lily, or some new discovery
of wonder and delight to offer me.
To pass the time, I started weaving this
rose crown for her, to fetch a smile, a kiss—
a simple gift, to grace her sweet return
it seemed, at first, but, as I worked, a thorn
pierced my palm's flesh, so that I threw it down;
another time a stem snapped, then a bloom
shook loose and wrecked the symmetry, and then
I had to start the whole thing over again.
At last, though still imperfect, it is done!
But darkness falls, and still she has not come!
Well, I'll go find her, and most gently lift
this thorny crown...

Eve (enters, holding out an apple.)

My Lord, I've such a gift...

Adam No! Eve! It is forbidden!

Eve It is done!

Adam But it is poisoned!

Eve Then poison is sweet!

Adam (the rose crown falling from his hand)

You have destroyed us!

Eve   No! I've gone beyond
the innocence that blinds us here—my act
of disobedience has cracked its shell!
Adam, the knowledge hidden in this fruit
is that our nature's boundless, infinite!
God, in His wisdom, placed the apple here
to tempt us, to ourselves! that we might choose
to go, as far as dreams and flesh allow!
But at the core of this mysterious globe
lie bitter seeds! with choice come good and evil,
with evil comes responsibility
for we have taken Nature into our hands
and must decide its fate—and, darker still,
with knowledge comes the agony of death
which other creatures cannot comprehend
and therefore do not fear. But, wonderful!
with death come joy and ecstasy, for flesh
is precious, being mortal—I can feel
my body ripening, grown tight and sweet
with passion, about to burst! My Love, come near!
this feast of knowledge is too much for me
alone. I need you! Adam, eat!

Adam   I must
choose you! though we and Eden fall to dust!

(Adam takes the apple from her and eats. He looks at her,
with new awareness, and draws back a step or two. The
stage is now in near darkness, except for Adam and Eve
who are spotlighted and seem to possess a radiance of
their own.)

Adam   looms on the horizon, radiant
angel or demon
of infinite possibility advancing

Eve   till half-blinded, trembling, limbs aching
to turn, to reach out
new leaves

Both   we stand, gazing beyond
whatever we are
or were

(Adam steps toward her again.)

Adam   About you ripeness hangs
             palpable, aching to bruise.

             Too close I could not breathe
             I would have to crush all distance

             until I felt that stain
             of sweetness flood my bones

             drowning in which I would drift
             forever, lost, blessed, dust.

   Eve   Now come, as to the rose
             comes the bright-bodied insect—

             what may grow
             is past this hour's unfolding...

             such stillness
             flowers at morning understand

             leaf by leaf given
             into the sun's hand

             (They take hands, embrace and kiss for a long moment,
             then kneel together.)

Adam   Like a packed bud
             rounding itself in the night
             its filaments poised
             at thresholds of sun

   Eve   or a great cloud
             of faintly-luminous dust
             suddenly caving inward
             to a star

 Both   the contours of self
             give way
             as darkness
             goes molten.

(They lie down and begin to make love, the light around them increasing as their passion grows in intensity, rising to a cry of ecstasy in consummation; then the light slowly fades to total darkness, except for the stars, which become more brilliant as the other light fades. Then stillness. More stillness. The starry vastness of the universe.)

VI: NIGHT

God (enters, dimly spotlighted, and sings to the sleeping Adam and Eve.)

Good, they have chosen
as I knew they would
the surging, ebbing
ecstasies of blood,
who were not cast
for immortality,
fleshed sweet as fruit
and sweet-toothed as the bee.

Well, they have had a taste
of Paradise,
my lovely guests in Eden—
no advice
that I could give would help them
who have grown
beyond me, to face time and death
alone.

They will forget me
and this quiet place
of golden light
and softly shining grace,
yet something of its radiance
will remain
to temper greed, lust
misery and pain,

some spark of love, compassion
like a star
to guide them, dimly
flickering, from afar...
Wake now, my children,
go forth, as you must
to try your great experiment
in dust.

(God withdraws. The stars fade, light breaks, and Adam and Eve wake. They rise and face each other, then turn and, holding hands, face the audience, as the house lights come on.)

INTERLUDE
1

THIS

unquestioned
unquestioning
mostly, as one cannot
stop and gape
always

reflecting in the middle
of the street, as the light
changes, must
get on with the business
of making it
across

cannot hesitate
to consider
the mysterious
beautiful
lips open, glistening
hungrily
to be filled
with light, cock, meat, drink, air

yet, moments
of awareness, wonder
that it's all here
that we are, somehow
happening, the privilege
unlooked for
wonderful, terrible
miracle

of this

GODFATHER

tough customers. Americans.

"We're gonna make you
an offer
you can't refuse."

a businesslike
ethic
of power

at work
in Manhattan
at Kontum
Wounded Knee

that has permeated
so much
of all we have accomplished

and proven
in terms of what we have
dreamed of
as a people, venomous

CHAMPION

It feels like coming
all over
all the time

endlessly cresting
ecstasy
through pain

the others
no less gifted
can't sustain.

REVOLUTIONARY AGENDA

(for Tom) what one must do
to make it
in one's field

and what
to make it
through the night

a land
where these two thorny blossoms
intertwine

JAN. 2

The living room
scoured
of Christmas

calendars
crèches
cards

that sugary
swaddling
innocence

of evergreen, swept
away with our New Year's
resolutions

we begin to breathe
again, feel
our flesh crawling

with anticipation
unadorned, back
to our lives.

ACCIDENT

Moving through days
events blur like spokes;
dust blunts the leaf tip,
skin cakes where the ring
rubs over and over—
we lose touch with blood.

Nodding in harness,
up ahead a car
swerves off the road;
the sun shies away
and people are lying
in an open field.

Weeks later,
talking about it
over a drink,
the front wheels keep spinning—
that smeared, gutted place
in the mind will not heal,

and still approaching
in the distance,
like a scream welling up,
come the fierce sirens
of helpless, unappeasable
rage and love.

HOSPITAL WINDOW

1   oranges, forsythia
bloom on the sill

2   mornings, the brightly colored
numberless little cars with their urgent
purposefulness
glide along the river's edge

all afternoon raindrops
merge, jostling blindly
down the pane

at midnight the gleaming
hives of industry,
a red light
like a pulsing ache:
Time, Temperature
Coca-Cola

3   oasis
Olympian calm
in the midst of feverish
progress

from which a dizzying
perspective
of what is of importance
should we return...

to rescue, somehow
something...a leaf, going under
the relentless wheel

4   rising at dawn to lean
above the river
returning slowly, dim
as health

drawn by the gulls'
restless circling

there is fear in the question
of what it means
to get well

II

A Christmas Oratorio
AND IN THESE TIMES
(for David Ward-Steinman)

PART I

Chorus   Drifting among indifferent stars,
ravaged by greed and battle scars—
a spinning ball, checked green and blue:
this much for us, this much for you.
O Earth, our mother! Earth, your child,
Man, has grown arrogant and wild—
war follows war and hatred greed
as if all men were born to bleed.

Bard   There are better ways
to live

worlds
within worlds

through moments
of radiance

difficult to sustain

and in these times...

Chorus   Man rushes blindly towards his doom
forgetful of the common womb
that bore him and the brotherhood
of life, because the light was good,
out of the dust—and still sap climbs,
love blossoms, even in these times,
and there is hope that greed and hate
will give way before it's too late...

Evangelist   *And it came to pass in those days, that there went out a decree from Caesar Augustus, that all the world should be taxed.*

Bard   Civilizations have slid
under, crushed by their own
magnificent stone heads
dragging the subtle
down.

Evangelist   *And all went to be taxed, every one into his own city.*

Bard   moments

flesh blooming
bathed
in a soft shimmering
nimbus

dimmed
by the conflicting
desires, demands, limitations
of mortality

blighted, obscured
by the expedient
abuses, perversions
of this or that system
we suffer, come to think of
as our lives

Evangelist   *And Joseph also went up from Galilee, out of the city of Nazareth, into Judea, unto the city of David, which is called Bethlehem, to be taxed with Mary his espoused wife, being great with child.*

40

Bard   as if there were no mystery
no miracle
in the clear fact
that we are here, living together
that we are here at all

Chorus   So many people on this earth
none of them enemies at birth
taught in the cradle that blind song:
"My race, creed, nation, right or wrong."

Evangelist   *And so it was, that, while they were there, the days were*
accomplished that she should be delivered.

Bard   under the familiar
husk
the live kernel
smoldering
suddenly blazing
out of the dark

PART II

Evangelist   *Now the birth of Jesus Christ was on this wise: when as his mother Mary was espoused to Joseph, before they came together, she was found with child of the Holy Ghost.*

Elizabeth   a window
open
so wide
stretching, she burst
into blossom,
light's touch made her heavy
with ripeness

so that the ghostly radiance
spreading its seed
inside her, for a moment
could not distinguish
her flesh from its grace
was just barely able
to tear itself out, reascend

Evangelist   *Then Joseph her husband, being a just man, and not willing to make her a public example, was minded to put her away privily. But while he thought on these things, behold, the angel of the Lord appeared unto him in a dream.*

The Angel   As when
amid strewn shavings
and bent nails
some spirit of grace
surpassing thought or skill
informs your patient laboring
prevails
until the work stands finished
luminous
and you drop, humbled, dumb

she is God's work,
and kneels in awe
to her own glory.

Come.

Evangelist *Now all this was done, that it might be fulfilled which was spoken of the Lord by the prophet, saying,*

Prophet *Behold, a virgin shall be with child, and shall bring forth a son, and they shall call his name Emmanuel, which being interpreted is, God with us.*

Evangelist *Then Joseph being raised from sleep did as the angel of the Lord had bidden him, and took unto him his wife: and knew her not.*

Mary His change
from disbelief
to reverence
was no relief

the vigorous, practical
man of the world
I'd leaned on,
so disarmed

my idlest request
performed
as if the Lord God
not his woman spoke

at night his fingers
brushing my face, throat, breast
like wild doves searching
for some place to rest.

PART III

Evangelist   *And she brought forth her firstborn son, and wrapped*
him in swaddling clothes, and laid him in a manger;
because there was no room for them in the inn.

Bard   always
here and there
in the rubble
among the fallen
wheels, helmets, shattered
stone limbs, heads

the delicate
flaming
of a leaf, a girl's sex
millenniums ago
still flickering
from the charred page

in porcelain, gesso, crazed
that apple blossom
milkiness
of a baby's temple

unwearying
flower of light

Joseph   Radiant Lady, love,
Mary, how far
since yesterday,
now everything we are
washes, is washed by light
from this new star.

Lifting him from your arms,
cradling him so,
I cannot tell
and have no need to know
where his warmth ebbs
yours, mine, begins to flow.

Chorus	Born of our love, our fears, our flesh in Bethlehem, or Bangladesh, a world of sun and rain and flowers divided into theirs and ours.
Evangelist	*And there were in the same country shepherds abiding in a field, keeping watch over their flock by night. And, lo, the angel of the Lord came upon them, and the glory of the Lord shone round about them: and they were sore afraid.*
Shepherd Boy	O! you should have seen the sky my father and I saw that night. O! as I lay sick with frost there came a great host in flight. O! it seemed the moon and sun had turned into one vast light.
Angels	O! Alleluia! Alleluia! —luia! Lo! this bitter night there grows a blossoming rose without thorn. So! arise and leave your sheep now leave them to sleep till morn. Go! and you shall find your king as frail as the first spring newborn.

PART IV

Evangelist *Now when Jesus was born in Bethlehem of Judea in the days of Herod the king, behold, there came wise men from the east to Jerusalem, saying,*

The Wise Men *Where is he that is born King of the Jews? for we have seen his star in the east, and are come to worship him.*

Evangelist *When Herod the king had heard these things, he was troubled, and said,*

Herod *Go and search diligently for the young child; and when ye have found him, bring me word again, that I may come and worship him also.*

Bard what had been conceived
as a land
ruled by the people
the republic
growing, becoming

confused
by size, sheer number
the intricate
machinery grinding, advancing
out of hand

lives mangled
the people receding
caught
in the relentless logic
of their own success

in the wake of empire
bands
of the saved, the eroded
going under
turning

46

> inward, back
> to the simple
> eternal
> light
> in the Orient

Evangelist *When they had heard the king, they departed; and lo, the star, which they saw in the east, went before them, till it came and stood over where the young child was. And when they were come into the house, they saw the young child with Mary his mother, and fell down, and worshipped him: and when they had opened their treasures, they presented unto him gifts; gold, and frankincense, and myrrh.*

Bard impossible to sustain
that feeling
of wonder, illumined
flesh suffused
with grace

**The
Wise
Men** Stiff from kneeling
on the cold earth floor
we rise, groaning, stretch and yawn
reclaim our crowns
and set out into the dark
from which we came

gossiping, swapping jokes, flasks, anxious
to resume the familiar
traffic of the world
where our word is law

relieved to let fade
for the moment, the miracle
of incarnation
taking place in the midst
of animal noises, smells,
our bowed gray heads
charged with radiance
jeweled with blood,
spirit flooding the body's confines
like a star.

Evangelist *And being warned of God in a dream that they should not return to Herod, they departed into their own country another way.*

47

PART V

Bard   Now, Christmas upon us again
its glitter, tantalizing
odor of pine and childhood as we enter
the glowing room

mired in the sickening
devastations
we have chosen
again and again

how shall we nurture
the tenuous, newborn
spirit of hope among us?

Evangelist   *And when they were departed, behold, the angel of the
Lord appeareth to Joseph in a dream, saying,*

**The
Angel**   *Arise, and take the young child and his mother, and flee
into Egypt, and be thou there until I bring thee word; for
Herod will seek the young child to destroy him.*

Evangelist   *When he arose, he took the young child and his mother
by night, and departed into Egypt.*

**Joseph
and
Mary**   I would go
where the fruits of love and peace
bow the trees
and the fields of friendship grow.
This land sows a crop of stones.
This land bears a harvest of bones.

I would live
in a world where truth and dream
have no seam
and there's nothing to forgive.
There nations walk hand-in-hand
in praise through the blossoming land.

48

Evangelist *Then Herod, when he saw that he was mocked of the wise men, was exceeding wroth, and sent forth, and slew all the children that were in Bethlehem, and in all the coasts thereof, from two years old and under.*

Bard how reclaim
from fields sown with napalm and steel
the lithe trunk, seared
in our brains
of a girl reaching toward us
naked, her flaming
stumps of hands?

Evangelist *Then was fulfilled that which was spoken by Jeremy the prophet, saying,*

Jeremy *In Rama was there a voice heard, lamentation, and weeping, and great mourning, Rachel weeping for her children, and would not be comforted because they are not.*

Chorus Someday, when, through grief, we've grown
to see all brothers as our own
the trampled seeds of hope and trust
may flower from the blood-soaked dust,
and parents bending at the head
of every newborn infant's bed
pour softly in each drowsy ear
a song of one world, deep and clear.

Evangelist *But when Herod was dead, behold, an angel of the Lord appeareth in a dream to Joseph in Egypt, saying,*

The Angel *Arise, and take the young child and his mother, and go into the land of Israel: for they are dead which sought the young child's life.*

Evangelist *And he arose, and took the young child and his mother, and came into the land of Israel.*

Bard how answer the star
still flickering, rising
out of the smoldering east?

Chorus Guide us, pure spirit, from afar
through darkness, stumbling, as we are
over and over to that place
where flesh is luminous with grace
and Jew and gentile, Black and White
kneel down to worship the same light
till our torn hearts and lands are seamed
and by love's blossoming redeemed.

INTERLUDE
2

2 WALKING

everywhere lethal
treasure—I said careful
put that down, that's dirty, that
could cut you, those
will make you sick—
he said look
at this one, what's this one
Dada, oo, well I want to
bring this one home

THE MEANING OF LIFE

(for Jim
McDade) at least that's the lofty title
of the poem I set out to write
this morning at 6:30
based on a dream I'd just had
that seemed to be saying it all

I'd just settled down in the kitchen
at my favorite writing place
the table by the window
with its two or three flowering plants
(the window still full of darkness
the plants looking half asleep)
and was sipping coffee and smoking
my second cigarette
having been interrupted
already a number of times
by Tiggy's comings and goings
(when he's in and wants to go out
his claws in your thigh let you know it
when he's out and wants to come in
he lunges at the screen door
and hangs there, spread-eagled, yowling
till someone takes pity on him)
but anyway, I'd settled down
and had actually written the title
and was zeroing in on my dream
when the swinging door swung open
and in walked Colin, my son

O shit! there goes my poem
I thought, but what could I do?
he's four years old, and I love him
and he loves me, in spite of the fact
(or is it *because* of the fact?)
that we're caught up together in this
incredible family thing
that tears along at a clip
of a zillion miles per second
most of the time we're awake
with rarely a thank you or please

so in he came, in his pajamas
all smiles, and wanting to sit
at the other end of the table
and spend some time with me

I told him about the work
I had to do, mentioned the poem
(he knows that I do that
though he doesn't really know
what poetry's all about
not that I'm so sure myself)
and said why don't you go get a book
or I'll give you a pen and some paper
and we can work here together
wouldn't that be fun?

but he didn't take to that
so we just sat there awhile
making faces and bits of talk
half serious, half silly
the way we often do
when nothing special's up
and he'd brought his twirly thing
we got yesterday at the circus
that lights up and makes a soft
low whistling sort of moan
when you pull the strings and it spins
so he was showing that off

and after a while, as it seemed
he wasn't about to move on
I poured juice and made him some cocoa
between hot and warm, with the spoon
left in the cup, as he likes it
and we sat and talked some more
about one thing and another
like why such and such is true
and how come this and that?
and what would you do if?
and can wolves or weasels jump
as high as a second-floor window?
and what do trees think about?
and I could feel my poem
slowly circling the drain

well, at some point I made up my mind
and told him I had to work
and that he could go see Mommy
or play in the living room
his bedroom, or the basement
but, in short, that he had to clear out
all very calm and friendly
but firm, and he'd picked up
his twirly thing in one hand
and his other was rubbing one eye
when he said, casually, Dada
do your eyes sometimes start to water
when nothing's hurting them?

I said sure they do, sometimes sleep
gets gunky stuff in your eyes
and makes them water a bit
when you wake up and start to rub them

then he said something else
I couldn't catch, but his voice
had gone a bit thick and wobbly
and he was trying to clear it
again and again, with no luck
and I was suddenly listening
and looking at him hard
and finally I said Colin
are you feeling a little bit sad?

his reply was all gunked up
so I said why don't you come over
and sit here on my lap
and we'll get all cozy and warm
so he brought his juice and cocoa
without spilling a single drop
and we sat there, rocking and rocking
not saying anything much
sort of blooming, along with the plants
and then the window was light
and Tiggy was yowling again

so we let him in and went up
and I washed and shaved and got dressed
and he went in to see Mommy
and then I drove off to work
thinking I'll try that poem

during my free block at school
if I can remember the dream

I can't but I've still got the title
so this poem, if that's what it is
will have to do, and maybe
it's closer to the truth
about the meaning of life
(if there is such a thing) than any
a dream could have given me

SCHOOL TRIP

Just off the canned rock's blare,
grating of steel on steel,
girl screams, and everybody
having a wild time—
I've walked a bit, alone
down toward the water, glimpsed through trees
and come into the cool, delicious stillness
of tall pine.

In the Arcade, a machine
where, for a quarter, you are the ace
and each twisting Commie Mig, when you connect
bursts like a blood-filled egg—
a stone's throw from there
chickadees and blue jays nest and call
through the cool, delicious stillness
of tall pine.

America, you make it hard for me to believe in you
even when you're having fun—
I see you on the Tilt-A-Whirl,
eyes clenched, mouth wide, hair streaming
spinning higher and higher and higher...
come down, come down
to the cool, delicious stillness
of tall pine.

Someday, if I bring my own kids here
and take them, hysterical, on all the rides,
before we leave, dazed, gummed with cotton candy,
we'll walk to this spot I've found
and sit awhile—
I'd like to tempt their dreams
with the cool, delicious stillness
of tall pine.

READING X

Stunned
by that bleak, unsparing
honesty
in poem after poem

that drives home the brutal
day you've just had at work
where nothing went right

your memory coughs up everything
you ever tried
to forget

failures
of parents, friends, lovers, marriage, fatherhood
agonies
of childhood, growing up, sliding
through an aimless, indifferent universe
in terror, toward the abyss

the unreclaimable
disaster areas
of your character
that disappoint even the cat!

Jesus! you groan
he's got me
by the balls—I admit
to everything!

Scourged of illusion
taking what's left of your life
naked in shaking hands
you drag home, under a darkening sky
of unrelieved anguish, despair
to find the house empty of those
who are supposed to love you
and sit down to write it all out
spewing image on image
of bottled-up misery, spleen
in the kitchen, glumly preparing
for them to come back and find you
purged, immaculate, bone!

They arrive, from shopping
first your older son,
four-and-a-half, unaware
as yet, of the change,
comes barreling, breathless, in
to demonstrate the new padlock
and chain he's got for his bike
he's just learning to ride
without the training wheels,
shakily balancing
as you run alongside to catch him

next the younger, the easy one
drifts in, in one sock, mumbling
a phrase from a silly song
you sang him the other night
when he seemed more asleep than awake,
and wants a big hug and a kiss
and a handful of Cheddar Cheese Goldfish

then your wife, whose shortcomings
would make an imposing list
almost as long as your own
if you set your pen to it,
sweeps in and lofts you a kiss
over the shopping bags
one of which has a giant erection
of Italian bread sticking out
that goes with your favorite dinner
of steak and garlic butter,
and not only fails to remark
the new, *real* you sitting there
but sounds more resigned than angry
when she points out the pellets of mud
you've tracked unthinkingly
again, on her kitchen floor

and seeing her, you remember
the movie that's on at nine
you're both planning to watch,
and that it's been 3 or 4 nights
since you've made love, and how good
how *goddam* good her ass looks
for a woman of thirty-four
who's borne you two sons, kept house
and on with her career

part-time, rearranging her life
so cheerfully around
the demands of a family
and you and your moody muse
for what is it now? nine years?
and how you'd promised her
to change the Kitty Litter
this afternoon, for sure!

And later, after you've scoured
the litter pan, bagged the trash
read 5 books, aborted 3 fights
been screamed at, fled from in tears
ambushed, ridden, devoured
resurrected, tickled, abandoned
for dinner, to lie on the couch
like the contemplative
eye of a hurricane
jotting down scraps of a new
poem that's starting to come
at just the wrong time, drawn baths
smoothed tangles, wrestled pajamas
spun a yarn from the on-going saga
of Karl the Kingfisher
(who spears 2 tin cans, a milk carton
3 leaves and a baseball cap
before finally landing a fish—
being, from birth, afflicted
with blurred vision, a fear of heights
and too much imagination,
yet struggling heroically
and generally managing
through it all, to hang on to his senses
of humor and perspective
as he gets up and goes to work
and returns to the clamoring nest
rain or shine, each day of the week)
tucked in both Snoopies, bent
in the half-lit hush to give
and receive the warm, moist, living
mystery of a kiss

as you're plowing through the strewn chaos
of pillows and toys and books
in the living room, downing a Scotch
digging Peterson, smelling the steak

already savoring
that pungent, buttery mess
sloshing around in your mouth

it suddenly strikes you that X,
for all his uncompromising
ferocious honesty
in flaying life to its nerves,
has missed an essential point
which needs to be made, about sharing
commitments, obligations
and working hard to support
each other, as best we can,
not just in those desperate times
of gloom, when the sun appears
to swing like a bloodied ax,
but through that ambivalent haze
of less spectacular
conflicts, triumphs, concessions
anxieties, needs, satisfactions
etc., that make up the bulk
of the day-to-day, long-term haul
we're all caught up in together
until the world fades and we
relinquish all storms of light

and how little X admits
of that other extreme: those moments
that come with a piercing rush
of tenderness, joy, love, grace,
whatever it is that fills you
till, brimming, you want to shout
obscenities at the stars
or smother the cat with kisses,
though you don't, as you might wake the kids
or get clawed in the face for your pains—
you just sweep up the plastic trash bag
that's waiting for you by the door
and growling, "Come here, you sweet thing!"
boogie out into the night.

INVITATION

nothing one can do
is ever going to be
enough, whether
as son, lover, drudge, parent, guardian
of the Word, the world
keeps coming around
for more, someone is always raiding
the fridge, or trying to
start something, or dropping
hints or dead at one's feet, and time is not
on one's side—therefore take care
to love yourself
not least, let the world look after itself
now and then, buy an ice cream, settle back
with a cold beer, take in
a game, get into the swing
of that ass, the sweet breasts
of roses, after all, one is only
human, a puff
of elevated dust, in that shaft
of sunlight the ancestral
bones are dancing

EASTER

Nothing. Good.
We are lost
and therefore free

to begin again
creating out of corrupt
mortality, a vision

of universal
kinship
in which light

each caring act
would outshine
the indifferent stars.

III

SONG OF ONE
WORLD
A Cantata at Easter
(for Viki)

"Being out of Nothingness...Life out of Being...Man."

—Thomas Mann

I: BEING

1 mysterious
issue
from nothing

eternity shaken
by event,
infinity challenged
by matter

that first inconceivable, evident
act of creation
when potentiality
leapt
into Being
space and time

the original, quivering particles
in the hot seminal charge
from the fathering shudder, explosion
into the dark, receptive womb of the void

breeding atoms:
vibrant, electric, chaotic, beginning
the whole tumultuous, slowly-evolving
festival of existence
out of whose growing complexity: everything, Man

2 but for the moment's few hundred million years
they were as children: self-absorbed, playing
their random, isolate games, sometimes jostling the
    others
here and there drawn into nebulous clusters

gradually, steadily, gravitating
into denser, more intimate groups,
more and more racing to join in the building excitement,
colliding, shoving, squeezing in toward the center
with its first obscure glimmerings of a new nature,
adolescents, heating up, flaring, under pressure
brawling, caressing, kindled to passion
their naked bodies on fire, orgasmic

the darkness retreating, the void giving birth
to a star

3 composed, a great nation
of atoms,
nuclear couples clashing, combining
breeding, evolving new forms
all swirling together,
the star settles down
to the long steady labor of maturity
spreading its blossom of radiance out on the dark

one of billions whirling about it
each nation allied
encouraged, restrained
contributing its voice
to the heavenly system
of harmonious interdependence

each galaxy one among billions
spreading apart
in the vast flowering of the universe

4 burning out, past its prime, after billions of years
the star gathers inward its fading petals of light

still evolving, its inner life grown more intense,
its core's blazing furnace conceiving, forging
new combinations, designs, of mysterious beauty,
its whole being suddenly flushed
with fresh passion, expansive, aglow—

but this last fragile twilight blooming
soon withers, decays
into a shriveled, dim, dwarfish old age

5   or explodes—

now and then, some fiery old giant
evolving still further, swells to spectacular brilliance

a genius star, whose immense concentration
compressing all matters, bursts the known limits, spills
      over
a heavier, more complex wisdom

dies, showering its precious gifts into space
for the new, still unborn generation:
the elemental building blocks
of Life

II: LIFE

1   light
      at the window
      streaming, the world
      awakening, spreading
      fresh honeys of lilac and clover
      clear, dew-cool
      thrush song, air rippling
      over the bedclothes, caressing
      the flowing ambrosial flesh of my love
      lying nestled beside me

      the two of us, thrush, clover, lilac
      are stardust, all one, the same atoms
      composed and arranged
      in Nature's masterpiece:
      Life

2   scattered elements
      spewed from the bursting heart
      of a star,
      buried in space
      slowly drifting together,
      atom by atom
      accumulating vast treasure:
      gold, carbon, oxygen
      all the essential others
      sorting themselves, reassembling
      fusing, arrayed
      in delicate symmetries
      molecules, flowering crystals,
      raw chunks of material
      massing, compressed into balls

3   on one of these neighboring planets
      circling a star,
      neither too far
      where all congeals into stillness,
      nor too close
      where a chaos of gasses seethes,
      an endlessly flowing variety prevailed

seas rising to clouds
clouds dropping to rivers and oceans,
rock heaved into mountains
mountains eroding to plains,
volcanos and weather creating lush seminal mud

Earth flexing its muscles
rippling its skin
its veins flowing iron and ruby,
basking, Edenic, ripening under the sun

4 somewhere in quiet tidepools, still puddles
warmed, enriched, sweetened, by sunlight
something new started to happen

as if Nature, bored
with the brilliant work of her youth,
inspired, bore down with fresh insight
into matter's potential

tentative, fiddling
sketching out, scrapping first drafts
of some still hazy, slowly-evolving idea

breaking up molecules, recombining them, linking
carbon to hydrogen, oxygen, nitrogen
on and on, forging more elaborate chains

coiling some up in tight skeins
twisting others in spiraling ladders
exploring, constructing the possible, rung by rung

bunching and packing whorled strands by the thousands
into a tough porous skin
watching them float free: dormant, primordial cells

brooding, alert to each quivering atom
each morsel absorbed and transformed into energy,
    burning,
the complex mass growing more and more excited—
chains snapping, links drifting, mysteriously
reforging, doubling themselves

holding her breath
as that astonishing moment of breakthrough arrived
when the first inert maze of molecules
stirred in her hand

yawned, stretched, and, shuddering, split into twins
browsed there together, swelled, split again, and again
till one of the crowd, a bit different
dissatisfied, restless
squirmed through her fingers, shivered
and dimly set off
on the long perilous, wondrous journey
to Man

III: MAN

1 Being at its most complex
profound pinnacle
of evolution from nothing
where Nature turned
to contemplate herself

slowly it rose, a vast cathedral
of atoms, molecules, cells
from the rock of everything that had come before,
the whole evolving universal community
block by block raising the massive, intricate structure
out of the mud, aspiring higher and higher
to that dim point where matter soared
to thought

2 from darkness, dimly
emerging
into the flowering dawn
of consciousness,
in Africa, millions of years ago

we turned things over
savoring, piercing their skins
exploring
sounds and gestures
to capture their souls

lion swelled in our throats
hawk wheeled in our hands
hill loomed in the sweep of our arms

becoming all things
in us all things were reborn
translated, woven, stored
in the skeins of our minds

stone chipped into blade
grass twisted to string
blade wound to stick drove into deer

flame leapt from our fingers
flower bloomed in our breasts
star glittered as eye of a god

and we, greatest mystery
godlike animals—
sensing our kinship, our difference
from the others
half-asleep in their furs, scales, shells—
feeding and breeding, stretching
the bounds of the known, the possible:
Adam and Eve

3   while our primate cousins roamed, day after day
monotonously eating as they went
stopping at night wherever they happened to be
in the shelter of trees, with full stomachs and empty
    hands,
we went out in parties, two or three days a week
to gather and bring back berries, roots, nuts and fruit,
or sent out our hunters with those of other bands
to stalk and outwit a gazelle, or towering mammoth,
returning laden with bounty for all to share

spending the rest in camp with family, friends
or visiting relatives in neighboring bands,
trading the latest methods, tools, and ideas
that we were forever inventing, refining, discarding
in favor of some new breakthrough going around,
devoting whole days and nights to dancing and singing
to the gods of the sun, rain, wind, or around the fire
under the watchful gaze of that heavenly host
weaving myths and rituals celebrating the awesome
act of creation, the miracle of it all

after a few weeks, picking up all our belongings
and moving along with the slowly-ripening seasons—

the concept of stealing, raiding, killing for gain
made little sense, with the abundance around us
and food that spoiled quickly—our meager store of
    possessions:
tools, hunting weapons, trinkets, that had to be carried
from camp to camp, were easy enough to make—
with nothing to gain from war, we lived in peace

and so it went on, for unknown millions of years:
small, intimate groups coexisting in peace,
    interbreeding,
Edenic in their innocence, still in tune
with the interdependent web of the natural world,
those most inventive, sensitive, quick to adopt
more effective ways of cooperating with others
in meeting challenges, threats, such as changing
    climates
or more powerful creatures, surviving to breed
still more intelligent others—gradually
spreading out over the globe, the ones who stayed south
growing darker to ward off the dangerous tropical rays,
those venturing farther and farther north slowly fading
to let the sun's nourishment in—but all one people
evolving their various cultures: Humankind

4 the Fall, that long-ripening, bitter-sweet fruit of
    knowledge
exploding a mere ten thousand years ago
with the breakthrough to farming, gave us new mastery
over Nature—we became her guardian
as well as her instrument, settling down to produce
and accumulate, with advancing technology
all the wonders and benefits of civilization

but also to hoard and covet our piling possessions,
raising armies for defense or something worse,
making slaves of our neighbors, trampling our brothers
    and sisters
on our way to new heights of personal power and wealth

tribes massing in nations, empires, ponderous blocks
eyeing each other with jealousy and distrust
through thickening clouds of fear and prejudice,
taxing the limited treasures of the land
with unrestrained breeding, wars, and lust for excess,
fouling the water and air, wiping out whole species,
breaking the atom, reforging it into a bomb

swelling in pride and arrogance to the point
where we, forgetting our precious legacy
as part of the creative cosmic web,
may choose, at least on this speck of stardust, Earth
that Nature's next act will be to destroy herself
in a great storm of global holocaust

if that should happen, the irony will have been
that the basic feature of Humanity,
the spirit of creative cooperation,
that allowed us to evolve over millions of years
cure diseases, turn deserts to gardens, visit the moon
explore the stars and the atom, and compose
magnificent harmonies of law and art,
enabled us ultimately to succeed
in the collaborative venture of self-extinction

for even the man who, on signal, unleashes a bomb
or lines up with his brothers to launch an attack,
whether motivated by fear, frustration, envy
a sense of duty, greed, a dream of glory
or the loftiest abstraction of an ideal,
is playing his part in a collective decision
that some other way of life, or shade of skin
or curvature of nose, threatens his own
and is his urgent mission to destroy

5 we have an urgent mission to create
from the universal atomic bond a state
of harmony, replacing war and hate
with restraint, compassion, sharing—it is late
but the spirit is in the long history of our genes,
the craft in our hands, the image in our dreams
to snap the chains of greed and arrogance
we forge as for our own annihilation

and weave a new song of one world, and a dance
in tune with the great festival of creation:
all nations whirling together, brightly dressed
in their various cultures of North, South, East and West,
each adding its note of brilliance to the rest
in chorus, out of the vast, collective breast
of Being, swelling in wonder, knowledge, grace
to praise the cosmic mystery of God's face

The Apple-wood Press began in January 1976.

The image of the apple joined with the hard concreteness of wood in many ways expresses the goals of the press. One of the first woods used in printing, apple-wood remains a metaphor for giving ideas a form. Apple-wood Press books are published in the memory of Harry and Lillian Apple.